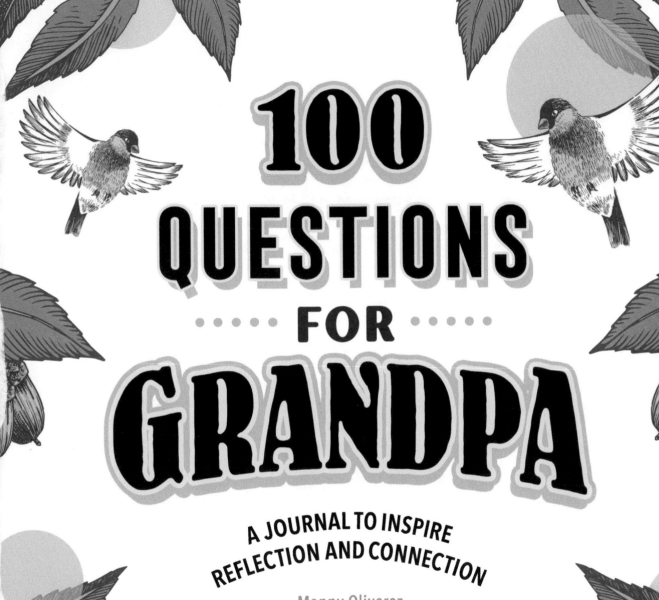

# 100 QUESTIONS ··· FOR ··· GRANDPA

## A JOURNAL TO INSPIRE REFLECTION AND CONNECTION

Manny Oliverez

ROCKRIDGE
PRESS

Hardcover ISBN: 979-8-88608-1-336
Paperback ISBN: 979-8-88608-8-281

Manufactured in the United States of America

Interior and Cover Designer: Gabe Nansen
Art Producer: Hannah Dickerson
Editor: Kahlil Thomas
Production Editor: Ellina Litmanovich
Production Manager: Holly Haydash

All illustrations used under license from Shutterstock.com

10 9 8 7 6 5 4 3 2 1 0

THIS JOURNAL BELONGS TO

_____

# CONTENTS

# INTRODUCTION

I never knew my grandfathers. Both of them had passed away before I was born, so I never got to spend time with them. I never went on walks with them, went out for ice cream, or listened to their fantastic stories. I never knew about how they grew up, where they went to school, what their dreams were for their families, or how they met my grandmothers. I never got to see them happy, hear them laugh, or even see them cry. I never felt their hug or heard them say they were proud of me.

I'm a grandpa now with lots of beautiful granddaughters and handsome grandsons. I spend a lot of time with them doing things together, going on adventures, and talking about life. I want to learn about them and share my life and thoughts with them. That was something I unfortunately never got to experience with my grandpas.

I wish I had a book about my grandfathers' lives. But that lack of information has inspired me to create and write *100 Questions for Grandpa*. In this journal, you can preserve the memories and stories of your grandpas. They will be recorded for generations to come.

I have sectioned this journal into five parts I felt were important. Part 1 is about Grandpa's early years. Part 2 is about his favorite things and values.

▼

Part 3 is about love, romance, and friendships. Part 4 is on what it's like being a grandpa, and part 5 is on leaving a legacy for his family.

So sit down with your grandpas and ask them the questions in this journal so you can learn more about their lives. Take your time. The journal does not have to be filled out in a day or even a week. The key is to learn about your grandpas. I'm sure there will be lots of things you will learn that happened in their lives you would have never guessed. I'm sure you will even hear a few crazy stories about your parents mixed in.

I ask that you savor the process of talking with Grandpa and asking him the questions in this book, and then writing down and preserving his answers in this journal. Feel free to come up with your own questions, too. It's all about spending time with Grandpa and learning about him and his life. I promise you will create priceless memories together that you will cherish and keep in your heart, and this journal, forever.

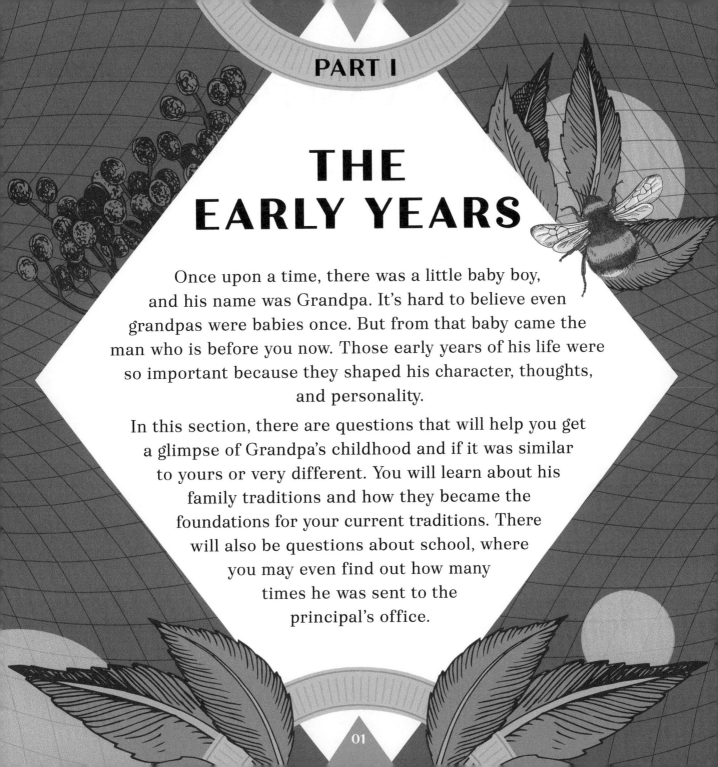

# PART I

# THE EARLY YEARS

Once upon a time, there was a little baby boy, and his name was Grandpa. It's hard to believe even grandpas were babies once. But from that baby came the man who is before you now. Those early years of his life were so important because they shaped his character, thoughts, and personality.

In this section, there are questions that will help you get a glimpse of Grandpa's childhood and if it was similar to yours or very different. You will learn about his family traditions and how they became the foundations for your current traditions. There will also be questions about school, where you may even find out how many times he was sent to the principal's office.

# — ORIGINS & ANCESTORS —

What is your full name? Why did your parents name you that? Were you named after a relative?

_____

_____

_____

_____

_____

_____

_____

_____

_____

_____

_____

When were you born? Where were you born? Did your parents ever tell you about the day you were born?

_____

_____

_____

_____

_____

_____

_____

_____

_____

What were your parents' names? Where were they from?

_____

_____

_____

_____

_____

_____

_____

_____

_____

_____

Did you know your grandparents? What were they like?

_____

_____

_____

_____

_____

_____

_____

_____

_____

_____

_____

What is your earliest childhood memory?

My family comes first.
**MAYBE THAT'S WHAT MAKES ME DIFFERENT** from other guys.

**—BOBBY DARIN**

# FAMILY

Do you have siblings? What are their names? Did you annoy
them a lot growing up? Tell the truth.

_____

_____

_____

_____

_____

_____

_____

_____

_____

_____

How often did you get together with relatives? Did you have a favorite cousin, aunt, or uncle?

_____

_____

_____

_____

_____

_____

_____

_____

_____

_____

Tell me about the place you lived in growing up. Did you have your own room, or did you have to share? Did you have a yard?

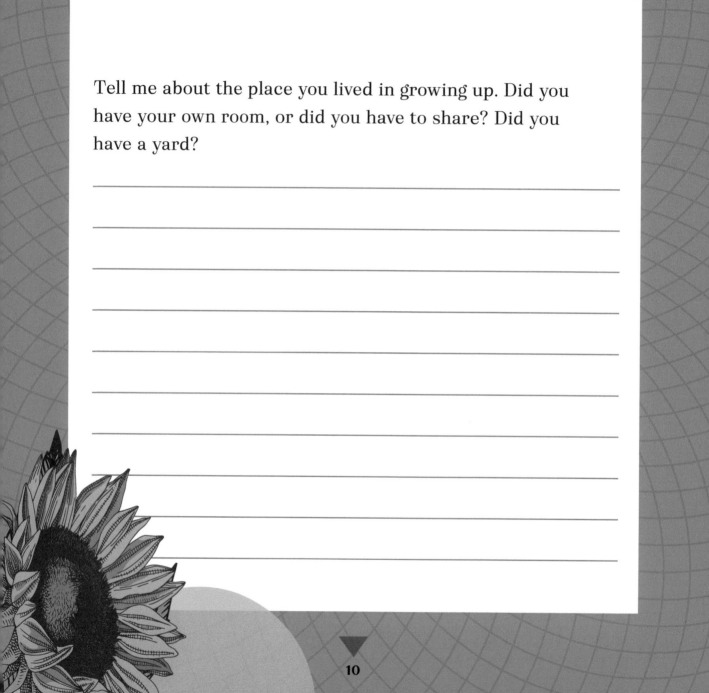

Did you have a pet growing up? If you did, what was their name? If you didn't, do you wish you could have?

_____

_____

_____

_____

_____

_____

_____

_____

_____

_____

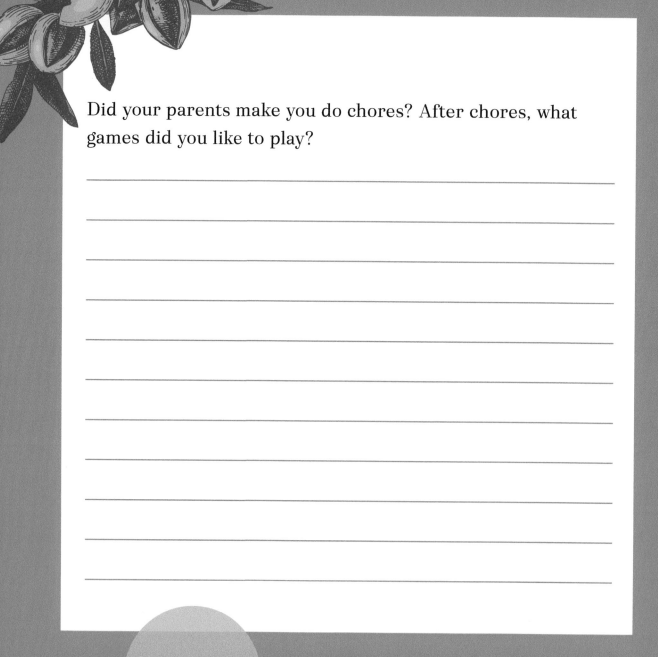

Did your parents make you do chores? After chores, what games did you like to play?

_____

_____

_____

_____

_____

_____

_____

_____

_____

Family faces are magic mirrors.
Looking at people who belong to us, we
see the **PAST, PRESENT,
AND FUTURE.**

—GAIL BUCKLEY

# TRADITIONS

Did you have holiday traditions? What was your favorite holiday? Why so?

_____

_____

_____

_____

_____

_____

_____

_____

_____

_____

_____

What is the fondest memory you have of growing up in your family?

_____

_____

_____

_____

_____

_____

_____

_____

_____

_____

When you lost a tooth, how much did the tooth fairy leave you? Did you get more money for a molar? What does that equate to in today's dollars?

_____

_____

_____

_____

_____

_____

_____

_____

Is there a family keepsake you have held on to? Why is it so special? What are the memories it holds?

_____

_____

_____

_____

_____

_____

_____

_____

_____

_____

How did your family celebrate your birthday?

_____

_____

_____

_____

_____

_____

_____

_____

_____

_____

I have the best memories as a kid eating ice cream. It was a **FAMILY TRADITION** that I had with my father. It was nice.

—MICHAEL STRAHAN

# SCHOOLING

What was school like back in your day? Tell me about a typical day.

_____

_____

_____

_____

_____

_____

_____

_____

_____

_____

What was your favorite subject in school? Did you
have a favorite teacher? What kind of grades did you get?

_____

_____

_____

_____

_____

_____

_____

_____

_____

_____

Were you ever sent to the principal's office for, let's say, being mischievous? If so, tell me all the juicy details. Inquiring minds want to know.

_____

_____

_____

_____

_____

_____

_____

_____

_____

Who was your best friend at school? What made them your best friend?

_____

_____

_____

_____

_____

_____

_____

_____

_____

_____

Were you given a nickname by your classmates? What was it?
Did you like it?

_____

_____

_____

_____

_____

_____

_____

_____

_____

**WISDOM**
is not a product
of schooling but of
the **LIFELONG**
**ATTEMPT TO**
acquire it.

—ALBERT EINSTEIN

# PART II

# PASSIONS & PURSUITS

We just asked questions about Grandpa's early years. Now he is becoming a young man. Grandpa has likes and dislikes, and he has started working and having his own interests. It will be nice to know about his life during those years.

In this section, there are questions that will help you learn more about your grandpa as he grew up. You will be able to ask him about his favorite things such as his favorite relative, how much money he made at his first job, and if he really did eat all his vegetables.

In the upcoming pages, Grandpa will have to reveal a funny family story, too. Maybe, if you're lucky, it will be a story you never heard before, possibly involving your parents, coming to light after all these years.

# A FEW FAVORITES

What was your favorite food growing up? Do you still like it?
Did you eat all your vegetables?

_____

_____

_____

_____

_____

_____

_____

_____

_____

_____

_____

Tell me about your hobbies. What did you enjoy
about them? Did you do them alone or with someone else?

_____

_____

_____

_____

_____

_____

_____

_____

_____

_____

Who was your favorite relative? What made them special to you?

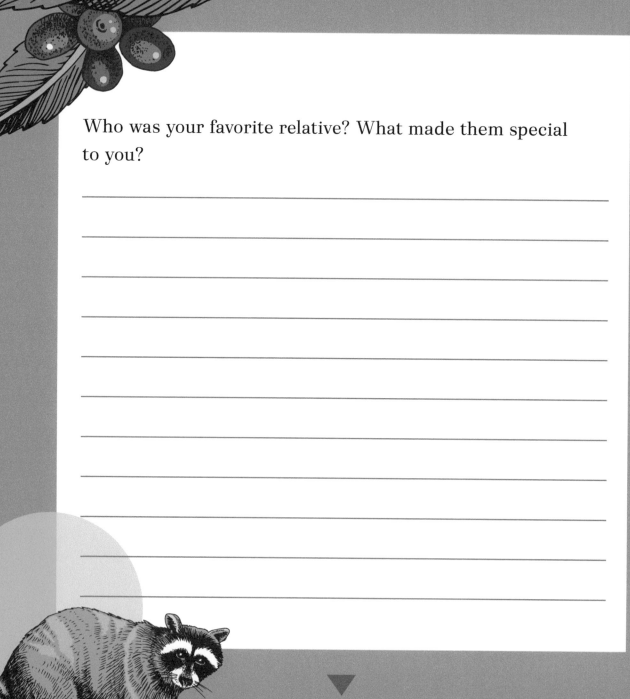

What is your favorite funny family story?

_____

_____

_____

_____

_____

_____

_____

_____

_____

_____

What was your favorite movie or TV show? What did you like about it?

_____

_____

_____

_____

_____

_____

_____

_____

_____

_____

" My FAVORITE THINGS IN LIFE don't cost any money. It's really clear that the most precious resource WE ALL HAVE IS TIME. "

—STEVE JOBS

# JOBS &
# OTHER INTERESTS

What was your first job, and how old were you? How much did you make? What did you spend your first earned dollars on?

_____

_____

_____

_____

_____

_____

_____

_____

_____

Describe any unusual jobs or bosses you had throughout the years.

_____

_____

_____

_____

_____

_____

_____

_____

_____

What career path did your parents hope you would take? Did you try to follow that path? Why or why not?

_____

_____

_____

_____

_____

_____

_____

_____

_____

_____

What awards and honors did you receive during your career?

_____

_____

_____

_____

_____

_____

_____

_____

What was your favorite job? If you stopped working there, why?

_____

_____

_____

_____

_____

_____

_____

_____

_____

_____

_____

**"**

Nothing will work
# UNLESS YOU DO.

**"**

—MAYA ANGELOU

# VALUES & BELIEFS

What is the nicest thing you ever did for someone?

_____

_____

_____

_____

_____

_____

_____

_____

_____

_____

What is the nicest thing someone did for you?

_____

_____

_____

_____

_____

_____

_____

_____

_____

What makes you happy?

_____

_____

_____

_____

_____

_____

_____

_____

_____

What are your most important spiritual beliefs?

_____

_____

_____

_____

_____

_____

_____

_____

_____

_____

What types of community service projects have you done?

_____

_____

_____

_____

_____

_____

_____

_____

_____

"

When
**YOUR VALUES**
are clear to you, making decisions
**BECOMES
EASIER.**

"

—ROY E. DISNEY

# NOSTALGIC PLACES & THINGS

What is your favorite place you've been on vacation? Why?
Who was with you?

_____

_____

_____

_____

_____

_____

_____

_____

_____

Tell me about your neighborhood when you were young.
What were your friends on your street like?

_____

_____

_____

_____

_____

_____

_____

_____

_____

_____

What is the most embarrassing thing you ever did?

_____

_____

_____

_____

_____

_____

_____

_____

_____

What game did you enjoy playing the most?

_____

_____

_____

_____

_____

_____

_____

_____

_____

_____

Is there a smell or song that brings back fond memories?
What feelings does it still invoke?

_____

_____

_____

_____

_____

_____

_____

_____

_____

# "

# IF I'M FEELING NOSTALGIC,

the first thing I do is open a packet of spaghetti, olive oil in a pan, garlic, a little bit of chili, a sprinkle of fresh parsley, and that's it. It reminds me of my mum.

# "

## —GINO D'ACAMPO

# PART III

# LOVE & FRIENDSHIP

Let's continue to reflect on and record Grandpa's words. This section is on romance, love, and the value of a good friend.

You'll start by asking questions about some of Grandpa's big firsts in his life, like when was his first kiss and with whom. Oh, and don't let Grandpa tell you he doesn't remember, because he does, and it probably wasn't with Grandma.

Next, it's time for more juicy stuff about Grandpa. We will ask him about his romantic life, ooh la la! He will tell you the story of how he met Grandma and if it was love at first sight or if he had to win her over with his charming personality. Finally, you get to ask him about dating Grandma and whether her parents approved of him or not.

# BIG FIRSTS

What is the first time you remember getting in trouble?
What did you do?

_____

_____

_____

_____

_____

_____

_____

_____

_____

_____

_____

How did you feel about having "wheels" and being able to drive a car by yourself for the first time? How old were you?

_____

_____

_____

_____

_____

_____

_____

_____

_____

_____

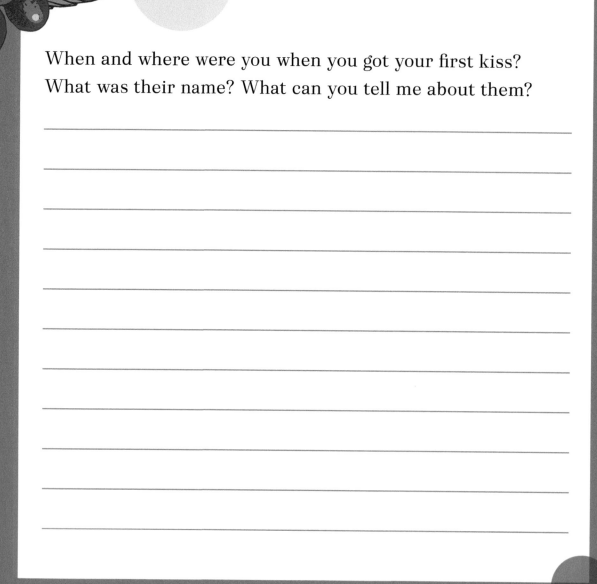

When and where were you when you got your first kiss?
What was their name? What can you tell me about them?

What was the first music concert you attended? Who did you go with, and where was it?

_____

_____

_____

_____

_____

_____

_____

_____

_____

_____

What was it like being a first-time parent? Were you scared?

_____

_____

_____

_____

_____

_____

_____

_____

_____

_____

_____

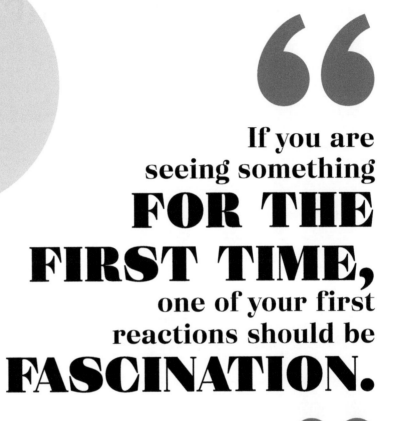

**If you are seeing something FOR THE FIRST TIME,** one of your first reactions should be **FASCINATION.**

—SUSHANT SINGH RAJPUT

# FRIENDSHIP

How popular were you in school?

_____

_____

_____

_____

_____

_____

_____

_____

_____

What are some of the things you and your friends
did growing up?

_____

_____

_____

_____

_____

_____

_____

_____

_____

_____

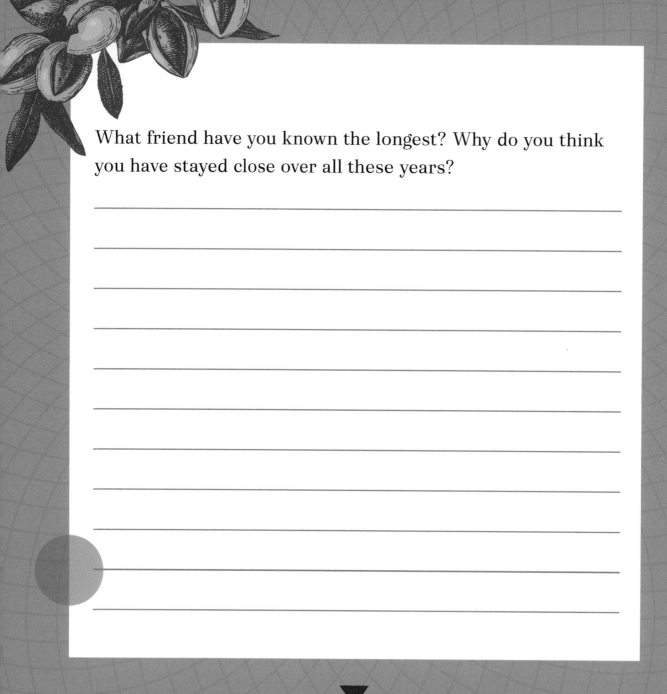

What friend have you known the longest? Why do you think you have stayed close over all these years?

_____

_____

_____

_____

_____

_____

_____

_____

_____

_____

How are your friendships different now from when you were younger?

_____

_____

_____

_____

_____

_____

_____

_____

_____

_____

Why are friendships important to you, and how have your friendships helped shape your life?

_____

_____

_____

_____

_____

_____

_____

_____

_____

_____

"

I cannot even imagine
where I would be today
were it not for that
# HANDFUL OF FRIENDS
who have given me a
heart full of joy. Let's face it,
friends make life A LOT MORE FUN.

"

—CHARLES R. SWINDOLL

# ROMANCE

How did you meet Grandma? Was it love at first sight, or did you have to win her over?

_____

_____

_____

_____

_____

_____

_____

_____

_____

_____

What did Grandma's parents think of you? The real
story, please.

_____

_____

_____

_____

_____

_____

_____

_____

_____

_____

What is the most romantic thing you did when dating?

_____

_____

_____

_____

_____

_____

_____

_____

_____

If you married Grandma, what was your marriage proposal like?
Where and how did you propose, or did Grandma propose?

_____

_____

_____

_____

_____

_____

_____

_____

_____

_____

Being the wise Grandpa you are, what advice on love and romance can you pass along?

_____

_____

_____

_____

_____

_____

_____

_____

_____

_____

The word '**ROMANCE,**' according to the dictionary, means excitement, adventure, and something extremely real. Romance **SHOULD LAST A LIFETIME.**

—BILLY GRAHAM

# MENTORS & INSPIRATIONAL PEOPLE

What teacher or boss impacted your life growing up,
and how so?

_____

_____

_____

_____

_____

_____

_____

_____

Who was your role model growing up, and what was special about them?

_____

_____

_____

_____

_____

_____

_____

_____

_____

_____

What superhero and/or athlete did you want to be
like and why?

_____

_____

_____

_____

_____

_____

_____

_____

_____

Who inspires you today and why?

_____

_____

_____

_____

_____

_____

_____

_____

_____

_____

Events, like people, can inspire. What event impacted
your life?

_____

_____

_____

_____

_____

_____

_____

_____

_____

The **DELICATE BALANCE** of mentoring someone is not creating them in your own image, but giving them the opportunity **TO CREATE THEMSELVES.**

—STEVEN SPIELBERG

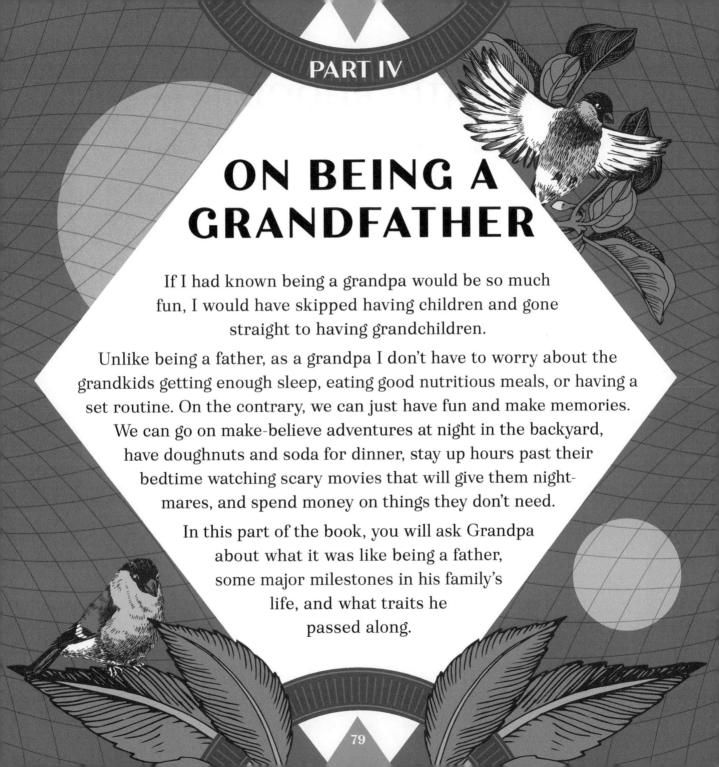

# PART IV

# ON BEING A GRANDFATHER

If I had known being a grandpa would be so much fun, I would have skipped having children and gone straight to having grandchildren.

Unlike being a father, as a grandpa I don't have to worry about the grandkids getting enough sleep, eating good nutritious meals, or having a set routine. On the contrary, we can just have fun and make memories. We can go on make-believe adventures at night in the backyard, have doughnuts and soda for dinner, stay up hours past their bedtime watching scary movies that will give them nightmares, and spend money on things they don't need.

In this part of the book, you will ask Grandpa about what it was like being a father, some major milestones in his family's life, and what traits he passed along.

# FATHERHOOD

What is your fondest memory of your children growing up?

_____

_____

_____

_____

_____

_____

_____

_____

_____

_____

What was the scariest or most challenging thing or moment about being a dad?

What did you learn from having children?

_____

_____

_____

_____

_____

_____

_____

_____

_____

Looking back, what would you have done differently as a father raising your children? Is there something you know now that you wish you would have known when you were a young dad?

_____

_____

_____

_____

_____

_____

_____

_____

Is there a piece of advice you would give to a new dad?

A **CHILD ENTERS YOUR HOME** and for the next twenty years makes so much noise you can hardly stand it. The child departs, **LEAVING THE HOUSE SO SILENT** you think you are going mad.

"

—JOHN ANDREW HOLMES

# MILESTONES

Tell me about seeing your child off to their first day of
school. How did you feel when you saw your child depart
for their first day?

_____

_____

_____

_____

_____

_____

_____

_____

_____

_____

What were your thoughts upon meeting your child's first serious boyfriend or girlfriend?

_____

_____

_____

_____

_____

_____

_____

_____

_____

Did a close friend or family member pass away when you were growing up? If so, how did it affect you?

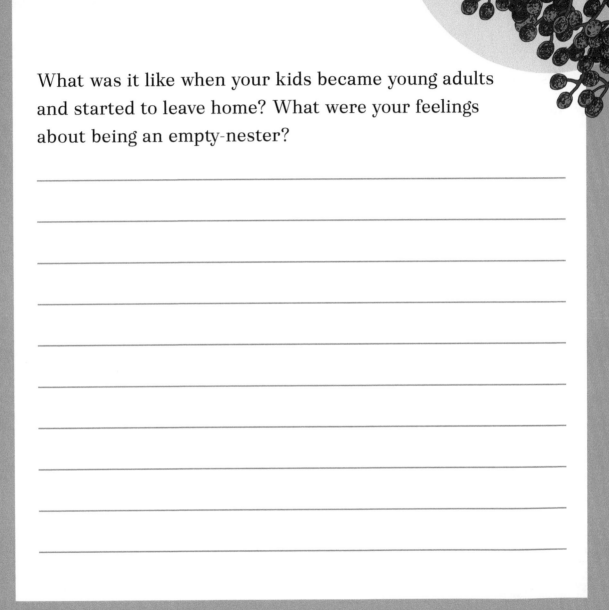

What was it like when your kids became young adults and started to leave home? What were your feelings about being an empty-nester?

_____

_____

_____

_____

_____

_____

_____

_____

As your children grew, they began romantic relationships, got married, and had their own children (your grandkids). How did it make you feel to become the grandpa and watch them become the parents?

**"**

# LIFE
isn't a matter of
milestones,
# BUT OF
# MOMENTS.
**"**

—ROSE KENNEDY

# BECOMING A GRANDFATHER

Where were you when you first heard you were a grandfather? What emotions were you feeling?

_____

_____

_____

_____

_____

_____

_____

_____

_____

Describe what it was like when you saw, held, and hugged your grandchild for the first time.

_____

_____

_____

_____

_____

_____

_____

_____

_____

What's different about being a dad versus being a grandpa?

_____

_____

_____

_____

_____

_____

_____

_____

_____

How do you feel when you are around your grandkids?

_____

_____

_____

_____

_____

_____

_____

_____

_____

_____

What kind of grandpa do you think you have been to your grandchildren?

_____

_____

_____

_____

_____

_____

_____

_____

_____

_____

" Nobody can do for **LITTLE CHILDREN** what grandparents do. Grandparents sort of **SPRINKLE STARDUST** over the lives of little children. "

—ALEX HALEY

# SHARED TRAITS

Do you share any physical traits with your grandchildren that you or your parent had?

_____

_____

_____

_____

_____

_____

_____

_____

_____

Family traits are not just about hair or eye color but are also, if not more important, about character traits. What character traits do you believe you have passed down to your grandchildren? Mention both good and not so good.

_____

_____

_____

_____

_____

_____

_____

_____

Likes and dislikes can be passed down. What are your feelings about brussels sprouts, and how do they compare to the family's?

_____

_____

_____

_____

_____

_____

_____

_____

Thinking about all your grandchildren, what are some of the things you have in common, such as artistic ability, love for music, etc.?

_____

_____

_____

_____

_____

_____

_____

_____

What habits do you have that you see your grandkids have, too?

_____

_____

_____

_____

_____

_____

_____

_____

_____

"

Traits like
**HUMILITY,
COURAGE,
AND EMPATHY**
are easily overlooked—
but it's immensely important
to **FIND THEM**
in your closest relationships.

"

—LAURA LINNEY

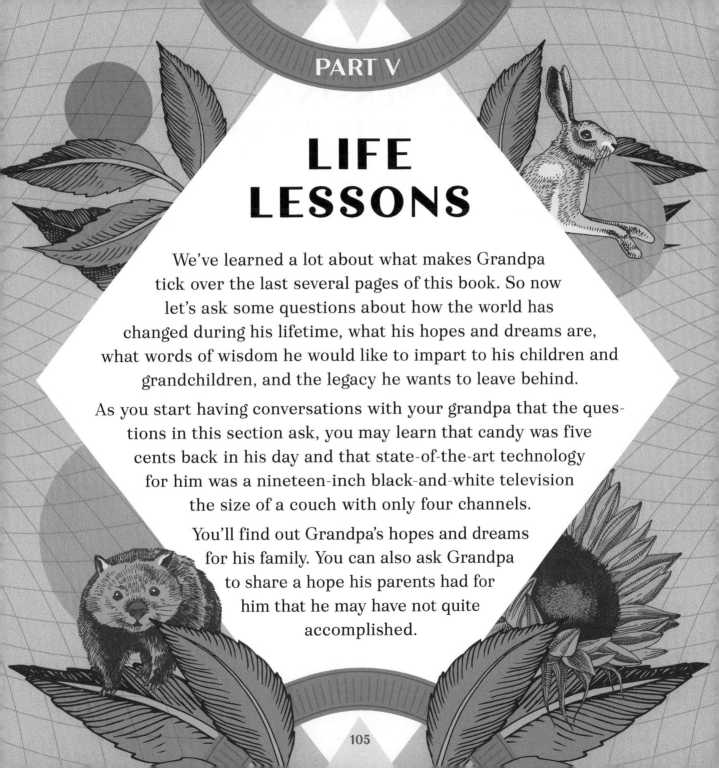

# PART V

# LIFE LESSONS

We've learned a lot about what makes Grandpa tick over the last several pages of this book. So now let's ask some questions about how the world has changed during his lifetime, what his hopes and dreams are, what words of wisdom he would like to impart to his children and grandchildren, and the legacy he wants to leave behind.

As you start having conversations with your grandpa that the questions in this section ask, you may learn that candy was five cents back in his day and that state-of-the-art technology for him was a nineteen-inch black-and-white television the size of a couch with only four channels.

You'll find out Grandpa's hopes and dreams for his family. You can also ask Grandpa to share a hope his parents had for him that he may have not quite accomplished.

# WITNESSING A CHANGING WORLD

Can you tell us stories of how much things cost when you were growing up?

_____

_____

_____

_____

_____

_____

_____

_____

_____

_____

What was expected of you when you were young? How does this compare to what is expected of young people today?

_____

_____

_____

_____

_____

_____

_____

_____

_____

_____

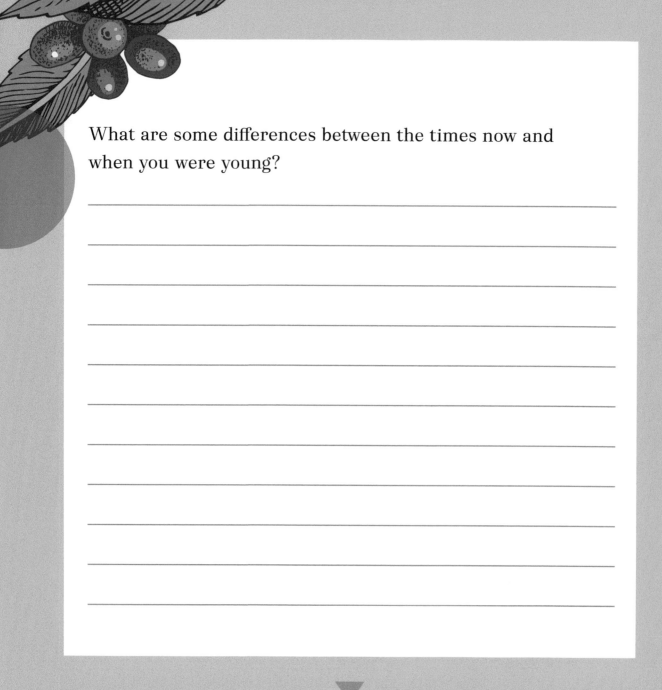

What are some differences between the times now and when you were young?

What is a world event that affected your life?

_____

_____

_____

_____

_____

_____

_____

_____

_____

_____

How has technology made an impact on your life?

_____

_____

_____

_____

_____

_____

_____

_____

_____

_____

**"DON'T BE SCARED** of the changing times. Things are **NEVER CONSTANT,** even if they appear so. **"**

—POOJA AGNIHOTRI

# HOPES & DREAMS

Have you lived your dream? How so? If not, what happened?

_____

_____

_____

_____

_____

_____

_____

_____

_____

_____

What are your hopes for the future?

What are your hopes and dreams for your children's and grandchildren's futures?

_____

_____

_____

_____

_____

_____

_____

_____

_____

_____

What values do you hope to see continued or stressed in your family?

_____

_____

_____

_____

_____

_____

_____

_____

_____

## What are you most thankful for?

"

It is difficult to say
what is impossible, for
**THE DREAM OF
YESTERDAY**
is the **HOPE OF
TODAY**
and the reality of tomorrow.

"

—ROBERT H. GODDARD

# WORDS OF WISDOM

What advice would you give to your grandchildren as they grow up?

_____

_____

_____

_____

_____

_____

_____

_____

_____

_____

What advice did you receive from your elders that has helped you?

_____

_____

_____

_____

_____

_____

_____

_____

_____

_____

What is one word of advice that your family passed down to you that you didn't follow but wish you had that we can learn from?

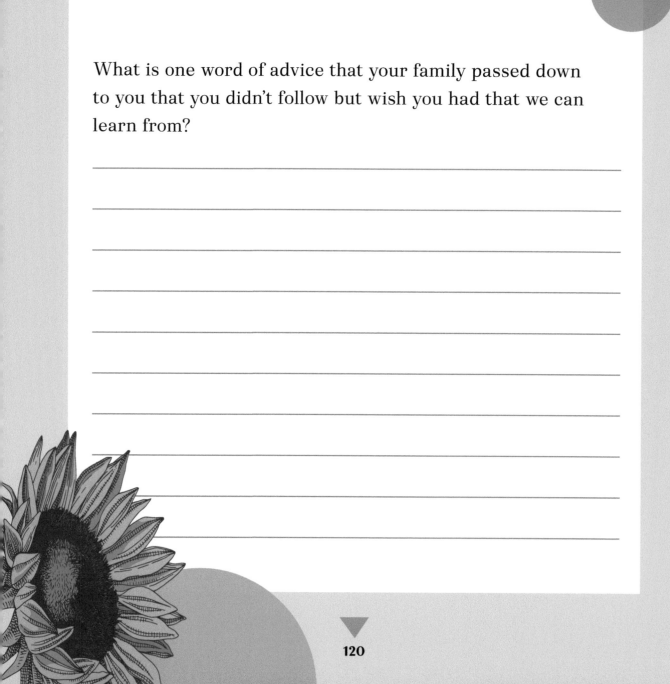

What have you learned from your grandchildren?

How do you view your responsibility as the giver of wisdom, a role model?

_____

_____

_____

_____

_____

_____

_____

_____

_____

_____

> **Be careful
> to leave your sons
> WELL INSTRUCTED
> rather than rich, for the hopes of the
> instructed are better than the wealth
> of the IGNORANT.**

—EPICTETUS

# YOUR LEGACY

How do you want to be remembered?

_____

_____

_____

_____

_____

_____

_____

_____

_____

What have you done in your life that may have helped others?

_____

_____

_____

_____

_____

_____

_____

_____

_____

What kind of lives do you hope your family will live?

_____

_____

_____

_____

_____

_____

_____

_____

Name a family heirloom you want to pass down. Why is it important?

_____

_____

_____

_____

_____

_____

_____

_____

_____

_____

What final words do you want to pass on to future generations of your family?

_____

_____

_____

_____

_____

_____

_____

_____

_____

The greatest legacy one can pass on to one's children and grandchildren **IS NOT MONEY** or other material things accumulated in one's life, but rather a **LEGACY OF CHARACTER** and faith.

**—BILLY GRAHAM**

# REFERENCES

Agnihotri, Pooja. *17 Reasons Why Businesses Fail: Unscrew Yourself from Business Failure.* Independently published, 2021.

Buckley, Gail Lumet. *The Hornes: An American Family.* New York: Applause, 2002.

Dukas, Helen, and Banesh Hoffmann (eds.). *Albert Einstein, The Human Side: Glimpses from His Archives.* Princeton, NJ: Princeton University Press, 1981.

Goddard, Robert Hutchings. *The Papers of Robert H. Goddard: 1898–1924.* New York: McGraw-Hill, 1970.

Long, George. *The Discourses of Epictetus with the Encheiridion and Fragments.* London: Bell and Sons, 1891.

Swindoll, Charles R. *Laugh Again Hope Again: Two Books to Inspire a Joy-Filled Life.* Nashville, TN: Thomas Nelson, 2019.

# ACKNOWLEDGMENTS

I want to acknowledge my loving wife, Grammy, who has put up with me for over five decades, has been by my side through crazy adventures, and without which there would be no grandchildren. I love you.

—Favorite Grampy

▼

# ABOUT THE AUTHOR

**MANNY OLIVEREZ**, aka Favorite Grampy, is a grandfather of seven energetic grandkids, a blogger, an author, and, armed with his old flip phone, an unlikely social media influencer.